THE FOOTBALLERS OF BORTH AND YNYS-LAS, 1873–1950

Borth United and the Ynys-las Gunners

RICHARD E. HUWS

2011

Borth football team, 1897

Back row: (l. to r.): J. Edwards, R. Hughes, Ted Hughes, W. S. Prosser, D. Richards, T. Richards, W. Smith. Front row (l. to r.): E. Ll. Williams, R. Roberts, William Stinchcombe, Price Haines.

Origins

Football was possibly introduced into northern Ceredigion as a result of the founding of the university college at Aberystwyth in 1872, but it might also owe its origins to the influence of the curate of Borth! Among the first recorded football encounters in the area, was a game staged at Borth on 2 January 1873 when a team representing the village, and captained by the local curate, the Revd David Pugh Jones Evans (1841-1897), played a friendly match against a team from Aberystwyth. The visitors could only muster seven players, but the home team managed to make up the numbers to ensure an even contest which Aberystwyth eventually won by 4-0 after two hours of play. The curate who captained Borth was a native of Aberystwyth and a graduate of Corpus Christi College, Oxford. Ordained in 1866, he served as assistant master at Oswestry Grammar School from 1863 until he was appointed curate of Whittington, Shropshire, in 1868. He came to Borth in 1871, and would certainly have been familiar with association football as one of the earliest recorded clubs in the world had been established in Oswestry as early as 1860. On that historic day in 1873 when football came to Borth, the Aberystwyth team was composed of players from the gentry and clergy and included Lewis and Richard Gilbertson, the sons of Richard Gilbertson (1818-1905), a noted Aberystwyth medic, and brother of Lewis Gilbertson (1815-1896), Vice-Principal of Jesus College, Oxford and founder of St. Peter's Church, Elerch (Bont-goch). Unfortunately, the make-up of the Borth team is unknown, apart from the captain. The popularity of football in Borth was given further impetus when Uppingham School transferred operations from Rutland to the Grand Hotel in the village in 1876-1877, following an outbreak of typhoid fever. Under its influential headmaster, Edward Thring, Uppingham was one of the leading football playing schools in England. Indeed, it developed a set of rules for the game in 1862, which were largely adopted

Borth football team, 1915

Back row (l. to r.): David Kenneth Jones, Harry Jones, David Gwilym Davies, Will Owen, Douglas Morris, Ernie Roberts, Arthur Evans. Front row: Leslie Mathews, Lewis James Herbert, Albert Rees, Tommy Tibbott.

4

by the Football Association in 1863. Throughout the mid and late 1870s more local friendly matches were played in the area, which all helped to pave the way for the formation of Aberystwyth Town football club in 1884. Borth played its part in this development, and an early photograph of a football team in Borth dated 1897 is among many historic pictures appropriately displayed in the village's *Railway Inn*, as one of the players, William Stinchcombe, was the son of Henry, the local station master.

The early twentieth century

Another photograph of a Borth football team, probably taken around 1915 during the Great War (1914-1918) has also survived and includes a youthful Capt. Lewis John Herbert (1900-1981), one of the village's most eminent and brave master mariners. It is also known that several friendly matches were played on the Brynowen Field following the end of the Great War by a team of ex-servicemen known as the Borth Comrades and later by a team known as the Borth "League of Nations". A team believed to carry the name Borth United competed in the Welsh Amateur Cup on 27 October 1928 losing gallantly 6-0 to Aberystwyth Town at the Smithfield Athletic Ground (renamed Park Avenue in 1934) in front of over 600 spectators.

District League Football

The commitment to organised competition dates from 18 October 1934 when the annual general meeting of Borth United resolved to enter a team in the inaugural Aberystwyth & District Junior Football League. Mr David Jenkins, 5 Britannia Place, Borth, who had been an official of the club since at least 1930, presided at this important gathering and after some discussion it was resolved to enter a team in the League. At that historic and significant meeting the following officials and committee members were duly elected:

President: Mrs Jessie H. Johnson, Birmingham & Birchfield, Borth
Secretary: Mr David Jenkins, 5 Britannia Place, Borth
Treasurer: Mr Cyril Davies, Ystwyth Cottage, Borth

Committee Members:
Mr J. O. Morris, Brynowen, Borth
Mr Jesse Cecil Mathews, Leronian, Borth.
Mr Isaac Pritchard, Gwendon, Borth
Team Captain: William J. Evans, 1 London Place, Borth
Team Vice-Captain: Clifford Jones, Wesley Cottage, Borth

The first league match was played on 20 October 1934 at Taliesin, and the first home match was played at Borth a week later. In general, the team enjoyed a good deal of success for the five ensuing seasons finishing in the top four league positions throughout this period, and winning the championship in a depleted league in season 1937-38. Borth United also won the league cup in 1937-38, and were runners–up in the following season. The fierce Christmas Day and Boxing Day battles with local rivals Bow Street are recalled in the humorous reminiscences of Borth-born minister of religion and former Borth player Dan Ifan Davies (*d.* 2006), who claimed that anyone who refereed this local derby deserved to be listed among the bravest men in Wales! Borth boasted several excellent players including members of the famous footballing Pritchard brothers, the Pughs of the *Friendship Inn*, and T. Arran Morris, some of whom played at a higher level for Aberystwyth Town.

Post-war football

The advent of the Second World War halted all local organised football and the District League did not resume until 1946-47. However, once the war was over some friendly matches are recorded such as the one played on New Year's Day 1946 between demobbed Borth soldiers and the Ynys-las military, which was won 3-1 by Ynys-las. Although Borth United re-joined the league in 1946-47, they failed to enter a team in the following season, but re-joined in 1948-49 and played for a further two seasons. They were then absent from the local league until they played for a single season in 1957-58. The Club was again a major force in local football during the 1980s and 1990s before folding once more in 2001. Borth United reformed in 2009 with an energetic committee and re-entered the Aberystwyth & District League.

Borth United, 1930-31

Back row: (l. to r.): G. Davies. H. Williams, E. Garfield, E. J. Davies, D. Lloyd, Harmer Goodman, John Butterworth, Samuel H. Johnson. Front row (l. to r.): C. Jones, George Pritchard, William Pritchard, E. Musty, Jessie Johnson, D. Jones, Jack Pritchard, W. J. Evans, D. Jenkins. Inset: G. Jones

Playing Fields

Prior to the Second World War Borth United played on the Brynowen Field, opposite the former petrol filling station on the approach road to the village, and now the site of a large caravan park. Borth United subsequently played at *Cae Bach*, a field which belonged to Ynys Farm, and which is located on the opposite side of the railway line to the former Welsh Congregational Chapel, and also on a field to the north of the B4353 road beyond Ynys-las turn. Later games were played on the Uppingham Playing Fields which are still used by the club today. Initially, the team played in claret and blue quartered shirts, but later adopted blue shirts.

Players & Officials

On the basis of photographs, press reports and registration records it has been possible to compile fairly comprehensive lists of both players and officials associated with various Borth teams from 1873 until 1950. Although the two lists contain nearly 200 names, they are probably incomplete, and may include some duplicate entries.

Please note that the spelling of place-names has been standardised and modernised.

Players

+ 19th century players
++ players recorded in friendly matches prior to league entry in 1934
*pre-war league players (1934-39)
**post-war league players (1946-50)
***pre and post war league players (1934-50)
Players with a Pantyfedwen address were students at the University or Theological College.

Attwood, Peter, The Very Limit, Borth**
Barlow, Tony, Stone House, Borth**
Beardley, Anthony, London House, Borth**

Bebb, A., Llys Dyfi, Heol Powys, Machynlleth*
Bowen, William, Queensville, Queens Road, Aberystwyth*
Brodigan, John Henry, 2 Hillside, Borth*
Brown, Bryan George, Pantyfedwen, Borth**
Buckley, Denis Hartley, Pantyfedwen, Borth**
Davies, Charles Henry, 1 Iorwerth Terrace, Machynlleth*
Davies, Daniel Ifan, Erwau Glas, Borth**
Davies, David G., 4 Cambrian Terrace, Borth**
Davies, David Gwilym, Nathaniel, Borth++*
Davies, David Richard, 26 Mill Street, Aberystwyth*
Davies, E.+
Davies, Glyn Ll., Auburn, Borth++***
Davies, Harry, Iorwerth Avenue, Aberystwyth*
Davies, Idris++
Davies, Jeffrey T., Pantgwyn, Borth**
Davies, John Ieuan, Glanceri, Borth*
Davies, John Wyndham, Brynowen Cottage, Borth***
Davies, Lewis, Glanrhyd, Borth* / Sidney House, Borth*
Davies, Lewis, Victoria Inn, Borth**
Dennett, Leonard (Len),Grand Hotel, Borth**
Duggan, John, Brynowen, Borth**
Edwards, Brinley, Brynawel, Trefechan, Aberystwyth*
Edwards, Francis Joseph, 3 Elm Tree Avenue, Aberystwyth*
Edwards, Ifor, Dolwar, Pen-y-bont, Dôl-y-bont*
Edwards, J.+
Edwards, Redvers, 3 Elm Tree Avenue, Aberystwyth*
Ellis, Edward L., Llwynhaf, Cambrian Street, Aberystwyth*
Ellis, Idwal++
Ellis, J.++
Ellis, John David, 3 White Lion Place, Borth***
Ellis, Thomas William, 3 White Lion Place, Borth*
Evans, Albert, Pomona House, Borth*
Evans, Arthur, Penygarn++
Evans, David Pugh Jones (*Revd*) +
Evans, Graham, Pantyfedwen, Borth**

Evans, John Alwyn, 34 Queen Street, Aberystwyth*
Evans, Vivian O., Dôl-y-bont*
Evans, William Denis J., Leri Cottage, Ynys-las*
Evans, William J., 1 London Place, Borth++*
Fowles, Frederick Bate, Vine Cottage, Aberdyfi*
Gardner, George J., Tanyreithin, Llandre**
Goddard, S., c/o Ynys-las Camp**
Griffiths, J. M., Minfor, Borth*
Griffiths, John D., 4 Cambrian Terrace, Borth**
Griffiths, John M., Pantyfedwen, Borth**
Haines, Price+
Herbert, Lewis James, Berlin House / Gerydon, Borth ++
Hoult, John, Maesglas, Borth*
Hughes, Glyn, Douglas House, Machynlleth*
Hughes, Hugh David, Boston House, Borth**
Hughes, Kenneth, Merlewood, 4 Park Avenue, Aberystwyth*
Hughes, R.+
Hughes, Raymond, Canteen Stores, Borth* #
Hughes, Rowland, 5 The Terrace, Borth*
Hughes, T. Clifford, Westbourne, Park Avenue, Aberystwyth*
Hughes, Ted+
Humphreys, Gwilym, Isgaer, Borth***
Humphreys, William David Rowland, Isgaer, Borth*
James, Cyril, Vaenor Street, Aberystwyth*
James, David Roland, Bridgend, Tal-y-bont*
James, H., Frondewi, Stanley Road, Aberystwyth*
Jeffreys, Reginald A., 5 Maesheli, Aberystwyth**
Jenkins, David J., 2 Beach Cottages, Borth*
Jenkins, Glyn, 3 Gwastad, Borth**
Jenkins, John Llewelyn, Dovey Cottage, Borth* / Ynys Cottage, Borth*
Jenkins, Richard Edward, 10 Poplar Row, Aberystwyth*
Jenkins, William Ronald, Ystwyth Cottage / Newlands, Borth***
Johnson, Bryan, Riverside Bungalow, Borth**
Jones, Clifford, Wesleyan Cottage, Borth* / Tyddyn Cottage, Llandre*
Jones, D.J.++

Jones, David Glyn, Gleaner House, Borth++*
Jones, David H., Panteg, Borth**
Jones, David Kenneth, Glan-môr, Borth++
Jones, Evan William, Myrtle Cottage, Poplar Row, Aberystwyth++*
Jones, George Allan, Gleaner House, Borth*
Jones, Harry, Troedyrhiw, Borth++
Jones, Idris, 7 Poplar Place, Borth**
Jones, John Morgan, Norwood House, Dôl-y-bont*
Jones, John Morris, Pantyfedwen, Borth**
Jones, John R., Craiglea, Borth**
Jones, Kenneth Septimus, Tŷ'nllechwedd, Borth**
Jones, R., 3 Maldwyn Place, Machynlleth*
Jones, Tony, Pantawel, Borth**
Leek, M[aldwyn], 1 Lledfair Place, Machynlleth*
Lewis, Robert Owen, 79, Maengwyn Street, Machynlleth*
Lloyd, D.++
Lloyd, Thomas Oswald, Beach House, Borth*
Lynch, Thomas William, Wayside, Borth**
Mathews, Jesse Cecil, Leronian House, Borth*
Mathews, Leslie, Leronian House, Borth++
Miles, Geoffrey, Hillside, Padarn Crescent, Aberystwyth*
Morgan, Raymond, Pantyfedwen, Borth**
Morgan, Richard, 7 Maengwyn Terrace, Machynlleth*
Morris, Douglas O., 9 Cambrian Terrace, Borth++*
Morris, Evan Llewelyn, Fron, Borth*.
Morris, John Maurice, Refreshment Rooms, Borth*
Morris, Thomas Arran, Belair, Borth***
Mortimer, Raymond Gilbert, Pantyfedwen, Borth**
Musty, Edward Thomas, Golf House, Borth++
Nayler?, J., 48 Copperhill Street, Aberdyfi*
Nicoll, Edward Edwin, 2 London Place, Borth*
Owen, Edward Murray, 10 Brickfield Street, Machynlleth*
Owen, Will, St. Alban's / Tynewydd, Borth++
Owen, William Ellis, 10 Chapel Square, Aberdyfi*
Price, W. D. Aneurin, 4 Wesley Terrace, Taliesin*

Borth United, League Cup winners 1937-38.

Back row (l. to r.): Isaac Pritchard, Willie Thomas, J. M. Morris, W. D. Aneurin Price, Cyril James, Enoch Pugh, Frank Edwards, Fred Pugh, Cyril Davies, D. Hughes, E. W. James. Front row (l. to r.): J. Hughes, T. Arran Morris, Glyn Jones, John D. Ellis, Iorwerth Williams, Victor Williams, Frederick Newton Stott, George Pritchard.

Pritchard, George, Gwendon, Borth++**
Pritchard, John (Jack) , Gwendon, Borth++
Pritchard, William Henry, Gwendon, Borth* / Bushbury, Borth++***
Prosser, William Samuel, Taliesin+
Pugh, Enoch James, Friendship Inn, Borth***
Pugh, Frederick Arthur, Friendship Inn, Borth* / Arfor House, Borth***
Pugh, John Lloyd, Friendship Inn, Borth***
Putt, William Lloyd, 33 Caerffynnon, Aberystwyth*
Rawlins, G. E., Cliff Haven, Borth**
Rees, Albert, Ynysview, Borth++
Richards, D.+
Richards, S. Rex, Sŵn-y-don, Borth**
Richards, T.+
Ridgeway, James D., Sandhurst, Borth**
Roberts, Ernie, Sabrina, Borth++
Roberts, R.+
Samuel, E.W.++
Sayce, W., Brynowen Farm, Borth**
Shaw, Glyn, Glanygro, Dôl-y-bont*
Speake, Francis Basil, Llys Eryl, Machynlleth*
Stinchcombe, George William, Borth Railway Station+
Stott, Frederick Newton, Neptune House, 9 Cambrian Street, Borth***
Thomas, Albert Ivor, Bronwen, Park Avenue, Aberystwyth*
Thomas, Arthur L., Seaforth, Borth***
Thomas, James Llewelyn G., Pretoria, Rhydyfelin*
Thomas, William John Kelsey, Pantyfedwen, Borth**
Thomas, William (Willie) David, Seaforth, Borth*
Tibbott, John Richard, Bradford House, Borth++
Tibbott, Thomas Albert, Riverside / Bradford House, Borth++*
Walker, Gordon J., Bushbury, Borth**
Wall, Stanley Maxwell (Maxi), Francon, Borth / Clydfan, Llandre **
Watkins, J. I., Anwylfan, Borth**
Watkins, J. F. E., Penymorfa, Borth**
Watkins, J. Llewelyn, Glanynys, Borth*
White, J.++

Williams, Arthur, The Graig, Machynlleth*
Williams, E. Ll.+
Williams, E. T., 10 White Horse Terrace, Machynlleth*
Williams, Enoch Gwynfryn, Mynach Cottage, Borth* #
Williams, Howard, Hyfrydle, Borth++*
Williams, Iorwerth G., 36 Brickfield Street, Machynlleth* / Glenmore,
    Llandre*
Williams, R. E., Malgwyn, Borth**
Williams, Richard Elfyn, Hyfrydle, Borth*/ Tŷ-olaf, Borth***
Williams, Victor H., Hyfrydle, Borth*
Williams, Vivian, Pantyfedwen, Borth**
Williams, W. Wynne, Lerrydale, Dôl-y-bont, Borth**
Young, Kenneth Middleton, Pantyfedwen, Borth**

*# Raymond Hughes (d. 1940) and Enoch Gwynfryn Williams (d. 1944)
are both commemorated on Borth War Memorial.*

Officials and committee members

Barlow, Anthony (Tony), Stone House, Borth
Butterworth, John, Brentwood, Borth
Davies, Daniel J., Erwau Glas, Borth
Davies, Evan John, Celtic House, Borth
Davies, Thomas, Pantgwyn (Vice-Chairman)
Davies, William Cyril, Ystwyth Cottage, Borth (Treasurer)
Evans, Richard, Pomona, Borth (Chairman & Vice-Chairman)
Faulkner, George W. J., Llys, Borth
Garfield, Edward, Mansfield, Borth
Goodman, Harmar, The Haven, Borth
Hughes, Hugh David, Boston House, Borth
Humphreys, David, Canteen Stores / Sea Haven, Borth (Secretary)
Humphreys, Francis T., Minfor, Borth
James, Evan William, School House, Borth
Jenkins, David, 5 Britannia Place, Borth (Secretary)

Goalkeeper Len Dennett in action at Aberdyfi for the *MV Camroux III* football team, operating from Ynys-las camp, 1943-44.

Ynys-las Army football team, 1943-44

Johnson, Jessie H., Birmingham & Birchfield, Borth (President)
Johnson, Samuel H., Birmingham & Birchfield, Borth
Jones, Clifford, Wesleyan Cottage, Borth
Jones, David Glyn, Gleaner House / Morolwg, Borth
Jones, Samuel J. J., Chesterton, Borth
Mathews, Jesse Cecil, Leronian, Borth (President)
Morris, John O., Brynowen, Borth
Morris, John Maurice, Refreshment Rooms, Borth
Morris, Thomas Rowley, Glenear, Borth
Pritchard, George, Gwendon, Borth
Pritchard, Isaac, Gwendon, Borth
Richards, D. (Maelgwyn)
Seal, Arthur, Morlan, Borth
Smith, W.
Spargo, William. St. Clare's, Borth (Chairman)
Thomas, William David, Seaforth, Borth.
Tink, William Denny, Cliff Haven, Borth
Wall, Stanley Maxwell, Francon, Borth / Clydfan, Llandre
Wells, Leslie, Compton House, Borth, (Treasurer)
Williams, Richard Elfyn, Tŷ-olaf, Borth (Secretary)
Woollan, Henry, Gwylan / Glanynys, Borth

The Ynys-las Gunners (1937-1939)

In seasons 1937-38 and 1938-39, the Royal Artillery 408 Battery Territorial Army, based at Ynys-las, also entered a team in the district league. Known as *The Gunners*, they also enjoyed some success on the playing field, including two home wins in successive seasons against their more illustrious neighbours. Although they finished bottom of the league in 1937-38 winning only three games and drawing one, they improved in the following season when they mustered a total of six wins and three draws. Their honorary secretary was Ronald Amos Wing MA, 8 Marine Terrace, Aberystwyth, a law lecturer in the University, and the team played in blue & red quartered shirts. Most of their 40 registered players appear to have been based in

Aberystwyth. It is uncertain where they played their home games, but the field near Ynys-las turn later used by Borth United, and noted above, appears to be one distinct possibility.

Players: The Gunners (1937-1939)

Albrighton, Fred, 1a Glanyrafon Terrace, / 5 Spring Gardens, Aberystwyth
Albrighton, T. A., 5 Spring Gardens, Aberystwyth
Albrighton, Thomas G., 1a Glanyrafon Terrace, Aberystwyth
Baxter, Idris Ll., Homestead, Dollwen, Goginan
Bland, Llewelyn, 8 Penmaesglas Road / 8 Spring Gardens, Aberystwyth
Brodigan, T. John, 18, Second Avenue, Aberystwyth
Cartwright, John William H., 10, Fifth Avenue, Caeffynnon, Aberystwyth
Davies, Arthur, 29, Fourth Avenue, Aberystwyth
Edwards, Glyn, 1 Beehive Terrace, Aberystwyth
Edwards, Tommy, 12 Glanyrafon Terrace, Aberystwyth
Evans, Eric G., Garregwen, Aberystwyth
Evans, George, 23 Glanyrafon Terrace, Aberystwyth
Evans, Griffith Lloyd, 18 Spring Gardens, Aberystwyth
Fraser, G. E., 10 Yr Odyn, Aberystwyth / 16 Portland Road, Aberystwyth
Freeman, Walter, Hafod, Bow Street
Goodwin, George Henry, 29 Glanyrafon Terrace, Aberystwyth
Hughes, Thomas Charles Elwyn, Gilwern, Tregaron
Jenkins, George, 19 Glanyrafon Terrace, Aberystwyth
Jones, Albert George, 2 Beehive Terrace, Aberystwyth
Jones, Eleazer, 15 Third Avenue, Caeffynnon, Aberystwyth
Jones, Harold, 2 Maesyrafon, Aberystwyth
Jones, Haydn, 7 Maesyrafon, Aberystwyth
Jones, Idris, 2 Beehive Terrace, Trefechan, Aberystwyth
Jones, John Iorwerth, 40 Cambrian Street, Aberystwyth
Jones, John Richard, Gwelfor, Banc-y-darren
Jones, Richard A., 24 South Road, Aberystwyth
Jones, Trevor, 15 Glanyrafon Terrace / 18 Spring Gardens, Aberystwyth
Kenyon, J. Frederick, 31 Glanyrafon Terrace, Aberystwyth
Laurence, Eric William, Langlands, Stanley Road, Aberystwyth
Livermore, John H., 17 Spring Gardens, Aberystwyth

Livermore, Percy, 17 Spring Gardens, Aberystwyth
Livermore, T. F., 17 Spring Gardens, Aberystwyth
Massey, Ronald, 12 Second Avenue, Caeffynnon, Aberystwyth
Meredith, George Thomas, 6 Princess Street, Aberystwyth
Newall, Arthur, 11 Glyndwr Road, Aberystwyth
Pemberthy, Frederick Ypres, / Linton House / 13, Fifth Avenue, Aberystwyth
Purnell, J. G., 2a Glanyrfon Terrace / 3 Glanyrafon Terrace, Aberystwyth
Roberts, George Vearey, 2 St. George's Terrace, Aberystwyth
White, John, Lodge Park, Glandyfi
Williams, John, 5 Grays Inn Road, Aberystwyth

During the war two separate football teams drawn from the Army rocket range at Ynys-las and from the crew of its associated merchant ship *Camroux III* played several friendly matches against other local army camps in south Merioneth including Arthog, Barmouth, Llwyngwril, Peniarth, Tonfannau and Ynysmaengwyn.

Borth United, 1948-49, League runners-up

Back row (l. to r): D. Humphreys, D. Davies, H. Jones, Enoch Pugh, G. Evans, Fred Pugh, Peter Attwood, T. Davies.

Front row: (l. to r.): Maxi Wall, Glyn Shaw, J. Griffiths, L. Davies, Student, J. Davies.

ABERYSTWYTH & DISTRICT LEAGUE TABLES
(compiled by the Welsh Football Data Archive *www.wdfa.co.uk*)

SEASON 1934-35

Aberaeron	22	20	2	0	153	32	42
Trefechan	22	19	1	2	126	30	39
Borth United	22	15	1	6	79	51	31
Social Services	22	11	3	8	50	54	25
Bow Street	22	11	3	8	50	56	25
Ystwythians	22	10	4	8	82	48	24
Corinthians	22	9	3	10	63	68	21
YMCA	22	7	3	12	50	60	17
Tal-y-bont	22	7	3	12	38	77	17
Waun Rovers	22	3	3	16	41	73	9
Padarn United	22	2	4	16	39	121	8
Taliesin	22	2	2	18	27	115	6

SEASON 1935-36

Trefechan	16	13	2	1	78	20	28
Borth United	16	12	0	4	56	21	24
Ystwythians	16	6	5	5	51	37	17
Corinthians	16	7	3	6	45	43	17
Cambrian News	16	6	4	6	36	48	16
Padarn United	16	6	3	7	44	41	15
Bow Street	16	6	2	8	38	44	14
Llanfarian	16	4	2	10	47	69	10
Taliesin	16	1	1	14	14	81	3

SEASON 1936-37

Borth United	10	7	2	1	41	19	16
Trefechan	10	7	1	2	38	18	15
Ystwythians	10	4	2	4	26	34	10
Aberaeron	10	4	1	5	12	25	9
Aberystwyth Town A	10	3	0	7	24	30	6
Padarn United	10	0	4	6	24	34	4

SEASON 1937-38

Trefechan	16	13	2	1	78	20	28
Borth United	16	12	0	4	56	21	24
Ystwythians	16	6	5	5	51	37	17
Corinthians	16	7	3	6	45	43	17
Cambrian News	16	6	4	6	36	48	16
Padarn United	16	6	3	7	44	41	15
Bow Street	16	6	2	8	38	44	14
Llanfarian	16	4	2	10	47	69	10
Taliesin	16	1	1	14	14	81	3

SEASON 1938-39

Trefechan	18	14	1	3	89	23	29
Padarn United	18	12	3	3	73	30	27
Bow Street	18	10	1	7	43	31	21
Borth United	18	9	1	8	47	42	19
Tregaron	18	8	3	7	53	60	19
YMCA	18	7	3	8	51	48	17
UCW Reserves	18	5	5	8	50	48	15
Gunners	18	6	3	10	51	66	15
Machynlleth GPO	18	4	3	11	37	77	11
Glandyfi Rovers	18	2	3	13	39	84	7

1946-47

The league was uncompleted due to a dispute relating to the use of several 'senior' players by various teams. Borth United finished in mid-table having won 8 games from 18 and drawing one game.

Padarn United	22	16	4	2	87	42	36
Trefechan	20	16	2	2	88	28	34
Aberaeron	19	13	3	3	82	35	29
Lampeter	20	11	4	5	52	36	26
YMCA	17	12	1	4	51	30	23
Machynlleth Reserves	19	10	3	6	55	41	23
Borth United	18	8	1	9	60	54	17
UCW Reserves	21	5	4	12	45	60	14
Neuadd Goffa FC	20	6	3	12	43	61	14
Urdd Aberystwyth	22	3	3	16	58	75	9
Bow Street	21	3	2	16	48	97	8
Taliesin	19	1	1	17	15	123	3

SEASON 1947-48
Borth United did not enter a team in the league.

SEASON 1948-49
(confirmed as the final table. The *Cambrian News* noted: 'As the resignation of Trefechan has not yet been officially accepted, their records are included.')

Division 1

Aberystwyth Rovers	16	10	1	5	50	39	21
Borth United	16	10	0	6	52	44	20
Neuadd Goffa FC	15	9	1	5	48	33	19
YMCA	15	8	2	5	50	36	18
Padarn United	14	7	1	6	39	34	15
Trefechan	10	6	0	4	42	29	12
Tregaron Turfs	15	4	4	7	27	38	12
Bow Street	16	3	2	11	34	51	8
Lampeter	15	3	1	11	21	53	7

SEASON 1949-50
Division 1

Aberystwyth Rovers	18	14	1	3	80	31	29
Penparcau	18	11	4	2	65	28	27
Trefechan	18	12	2	4	66	35	26
YMCA	18	10	1	7	41	38	21
Bow Street	18	8	2	8	58	55	18
Tal-y-bont	18	7	2	9	64	75	16
Tregaron Turfs	18	7	1	10	49	45	15
British Rail	18	6	3	10	50	52	13
Borth United	18	4	2	12	28	71	10
Padarn United	18	1	1	16	31	97	3

Bibliography & Acknowledgements

Aberystwyth & District Football League minutes and the files of the *Borth Review, Cambrian News, Welsh Gazette* and *Y Tincer* deposited at the National Library of Wales; Cardiganshire electoral registers deposited at the National Library and Ceredigion Archives.

The league tables posted on the website of the Welsh Football Data Archive: **www.wfda.co.uk**. Grateful thanks to Mel ab Ior Thomas, Blaenau Ffestiniog for his permission to reproduce them in this booklet.

Dan Ifan Davies: *Tua'r lle bu dechre'r daith*, (1983).

Gwyn Jenkins: *A history of the Aberystwyth & District Football League,* (1984).

Peter Parry, Brian Lile & Donald Griffiths: *The Old Black & Green: Aberystwyth Town Football Club, 1884-1984,* (1987).

I am also very grateful to the staff at the National Library of Wales, Llyfrgell Ceredigion and Ceredigion Archives for their assistance. I would also like to thank Mrs Jean Caswell, Marlborough, Wiltshire for providing the 1915 photograph, Mr Len Dennett of Borth for permission to reproduce the photographs of the Ynys-las Army and *MV Camroux III* teams and Mr J. Hywel Owen, Railway Inn, Borth for his permission to reproduce several photographs from his collection. Thanks are also due to Miss Ann Budge, Mr Peter Fleming, Mrs Eirwen Owen, and Mr Graham Taylor of Borth, Mr Gil Jones, Llandre, Mr Owain Hammonds, Bont-goch, Mr Medwyn Parry, RCAHM Wales, and the Revd Dr David Williams, Aberystwyth for their valuable assistance.

Printed by Y Lolfa, Tal-y-bont and published in 2011 by the author, Richard E. Huws, Pantgwyn, Bont-goch (Elerch), Ceredigion. SY24 5DP. rehuws@aol.com